FLEET AIR ARM 1920–1939

Ray Sturtivant

Front cover illustration: An early photograph of the second production example of the Fairey Seal (K3478) flying over HMS *Courageous*, with a destroyer in attendance in the distance. The photograph was taken during the Home Fleet Summer Cruise in May 1933, and the aircraft was then serving with the recently formed No. 821 (Spotter Reconnaissance) Squadron, being later adorned with the fleet number '731'. (RAF Museum P.101720)

Back cover illustrations:
Top: Fairey Flycatcher S1289, of No. 405 (Fleet Fighter) Flight, equipped with white-painted wooden floats, flies over the Fleet in Gibraltar harbour around March 1930. The aircraft's fleet number, '16', is carried on the white-edged red diagonal band of HMS *Furious*. (RAF Museum P.100922)

Bottom. Hawker Ospreys of No. 800 (Fleet Fighter) Squadron lined up for take-off from HMS *Ark Royal* early in 1939. The first machine is just departing, its undercarriage partially obscured by the smoke streamer. The ship's arrester wires are plainly seen stretched across the flight deck. (RAF Museum P.194823)

1. Fairey Seal K4207 of No. 821 (Spotter Reconnaissance) Squadron from HMS *Courageous* flying over the Fleet off Gibraltar, probably in March 1935. The aircraft is fitted with metal floats, and its fleet number, '735', is painted on a light blue diagonal fuselage band. (RAF Museum P.102197)

FLEET AIR ARM 1920–1939

Ray Sturtivant

ARMS AND
ARMOUR

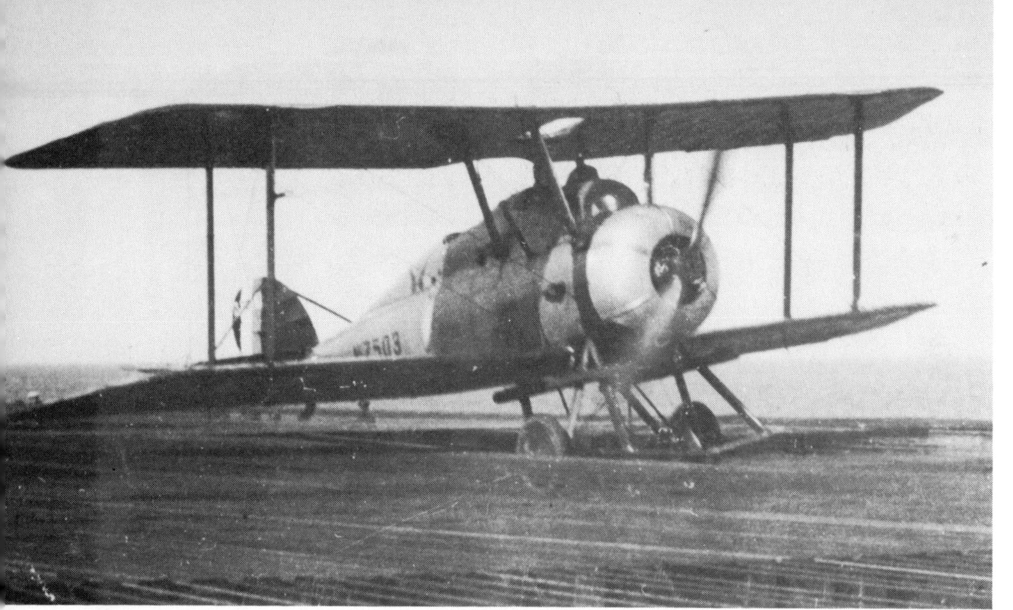

▲2

▲3 ▼4

2. Although ordered during the closing stages of the First World War, the Parnall Panther fleet reconnaissance aircraft did not enter full service until 1920–21. This example, N7503, served with No. 205 (Fleet Reconnaissance) Flight and is seen here aboard HMS *Argus*. Visible in the foreground are the early fore-and-aft deck wires, designed to make an aircraft keep straight and stop it from going over the side. The wires could be dangerous, however, if the aircraft drifted while landing. (RAF Museum P.1529)

3. A number of Gloster Nightjar served with No. 203 (Fleet Fighter) Squadron in Turkey during the last three months of 1922, during the Chanak crisis; they used Kilya Bay as a base, as seen here in November of that year. Shipped out in HMS *Argus* the squadron personnel found conditions somewhat primitive, only tented accommodation being available despite the onse of winter. The following April th squadron was split, the main pa becoming No. 402 (Fleet Fighter) Flight for service in HMS *Argus*. (G. S. Leslie/J. M. Bruce collection)

4. Gloster Nightjar H8540 was one of a small number of aircra of this type converted from lat wartime built Nieuport Nighthawk day fighters to become fle fighters. This particular exampl probably photographed at Leuchars, is known to have served with No. 401 (Fleet Fighter) Flight aboard HMS *Argus* during the summer of 1923. (G. S. Leslie/J. M. Bruce collection)

INTRODUCTION

First published in Great Britain in 1990 by Arms and Armour Press, Artillery House, Artillery Row, London SW1P 1RT.

Distributed in the USA by Sterling Publishing Co. Inc., 387 Park Avenue South, New York, NY 10016–8810.

Distributed in Australia by Capricorn Link (Australia) Pty. Ltd, P.O. Box 665, Lane Cove, New South Wales 2066, Australia.

British Library Cataloguing in Publication Data
Sturtivant, Ray
Fleet Air Arm 1920–1939.
(Vintage aviation fotofax).
1. Great Britain. Royal Navy.
Fleet Air Arm, history
I. Title
358.4'00941
ISBN 0-85409-054-2

Line illustrations by Mike Keep.

Designed and edited by DAG Publications Ltd. Designed by David Gibbons; edited by Roger Chesneau; layout by Cilla Eurich; typeset by Ronset Typesetters Ltd, Darwen, Lancashire, and Typesetters (Birmingham) Ltd, Warley, West Midlands; camera-work by M&E Reproductions, North Fambridge, Essex; printed and bound in Great Britain by The Alden Press, Oxford.

On 1 April 1918 the Royal Naval Air Service was absorbed into the newly formed Royal Air Force. By that stage the RNAS had grown to a large force, with numerous air stations around the British coast and also around the Mediterranean and Aegean, and flew a varied collection of landplanes, floatplanes and lighter-than-air craft. In addition, several squadrons equipped with modern fighters and bombers were operating alongside the Royal Flying Corps on the Western Front. At the time of the change, these units had '200' added to their squadron numbers, to avoid clashing with similarly numbered RFC units, and other naval operational air units and stations were also given squadron numbers in the '200' series.

At the end of the First World War the naval element of the RAF was run down rapidly, only a small nucleus being retained. The coastal squadrons, equipped with floatplanes and flying boats, and retaining '200' series numbers, were put under a new Coastal Area, later to become Coastal Command. With one exception '200' series squadron numbers were also allotted to the four squadrons formed for operation from the new aircraft carriers. Nos. 203, 205 and 210 Squadrons, and later No. 3 Squadron, were initially equipped with wartime Sopwith Camels, DH9As, Parnall Panthers and Sopwith Cuckoos, but these gradually gave way to postwar Westland Walruses, Gloster Nightjars and Blackburn Darts.

On 1 April 1923 the carrier units were given identities separate from the normal RAF squadrons. The four carrier squadrons were broken up into flights of six aircraft, each numbered in a new '400' series, which itself was sub-divided, numbers 401 onwards being reserved for Fleet Fighter flights, 420 onwards for Fleet Spotter flights, 440 onwards for Fleet Reconnaissance flights and 460 onwards for Fleet Torpedo flights. A year later these units became officially known collectively as the Fleet Air Arm of the Royal Air Force, and the term 'Fleet Air Arm' has survived to the present day. Aircraft of this period adopted colourful markings, many examples of which are illustrated and described in the following pages.

The number of flights allocated to each carrier depended on the ship's size, HMS *Hermes*, for instance, being able to take only two flights whereas HMS *Courageous*, when she appeared in 1928, could take up to nine flights. Equipment gradually progressed through such types as the Fairey Flycatcher, Blackburn Blackburn and Fairey IIIDs and IIIFs to Hawker Nimrods and Ospreys, Blackburn Ripons and Darts and Fairey Seals and Swordfish. Shortly before the Second World War the first naval monoplane, the Blackburn Skua, appeared.

Most of these flights operated from carriers based in home waters, with shore bases at Gosport and Leuchars. There was, however, generally one carrier serving with the Mediterranean Fleet, its aircraft using Hal Far, Malta, as a shore base, and another on the China Station, using Kai Tak aerodrome, Hong Kong, in the winter and the more northerly Wei-hai-Wei in the summer, floats being necessary at the latter because there was no shore base.

An increasing number of naval aircraft were also operated from large warships. Initially flown from wooden platforms fixed on top of the ships' main turrets, these were gradually superseded by catapults fired by either compressed air or cordite.

Various types of aircraft were used for this purpose, some flights ultimately being earmarked specifically for this type of operation. The latter retained their '400' series numbers in April 1933, when the 27 carrier based flights were reorganized into larger units, these being given squadron status and numbered in a new '800' series. It was not until July 1936 that the '400' series was finally abandoned, the flights reserved for catapult operation having by then become rather unwieldy in size with the increasing number of catapult-equipped cruisers and battleships. They were broken up to form a new '700' series of catapult flights.

Life in the peacetime Fleet Air Arm was largely one of trips to sea for practice flights and deck landings, with the occasional exercise and various cruises. On occasion they were called upon during a time of crisis, for instance in Turkey in 1922, China in 1927, Palestine in 1929 and Abyssinia in 1935. They also helped to combat pirate raids in Chinese waters. By 1939, however, they were preparing for the much more active role which lay ahead.

At just this time, the Royal Navy finally succeeded in its twenty-year campaign to regain its air arm. On 24 May 1939 it took over from the RAF the administration and control of the men, machines and stations of the Fleet Air Arm under the 'Inskip Award'. It gained several new shore bases, all of which were given ship's names in naval tradition, and set up at these its own series of training and support units. Unlike RAF practice, all these second-line units were given squadron status, being allocated vacant numbers in the '700' series. By the time the Second World War broke out on 3 September 1939 there were seven carriers in commission and the FAA had sixteen first-line squadrons, eleven catapult squadrons, a seaplane squadron and eleven second-line squadrons. This number was to be greatly expanded in the years ahead.

5. An early example of the Blackburn Blackburn I, N9581 was displayed in the New Types Park at the annual RAF Display at Hendon in June 1923 and bears the number '5' for the occasion. In this variant, petrol tanks were carried on top of the upper wings, which were connected directly to the upper fuselage. This particular machine later served with No. 420 (Fleet Spotter) Flight aboard HMS *Furious*.

6. The Parnall Plover was a direct competitor to the Fairey Flycatcher, but production was limited to eighteen machines, only Nos. 403 and 404 (Fleet Fighter) Flights receiving them before they were withdrawn. The type was found to suffer from some structural weakness, and with the success of the Flycatcher there was no great incentive to devote much effort to curing this. N9702 is here seen at Martlesham Heath. (Official)

▼5

7. Blackburn Dart N9551, of No. 210 (Torpedo Bomber) Squadron, taking off from the flight deck of HMS *Argus* on 9 March 1923 with Lieutenant Dally at the controls. Clearly seen are the fore-and-aft deck wires in vogue at that time to help the aircraft maintain a straight course after landing. Inside each main wheel of the aircraft is a Bryer hook for picking up these wires. (FAA Museum)

8. No. 440 (Fleet Reconnaissance) Flight was the only unit to be fully equipped with the Supermarine Seagull III amphibian flying boat. The type proved unsatisfactory, and was replaced in the flight by Fairey IIIDs in January 1925, but it laid the foundation for the later Seagull V, which became the highly successful Walrus. The flight was attached to HMS *Eagle*, and N9647 '41', seen here over the coast of Malta, has the typical varnished mahogany fuselage with white hull and fleet number, the wings being silver.

6▲

7▲ 8▼

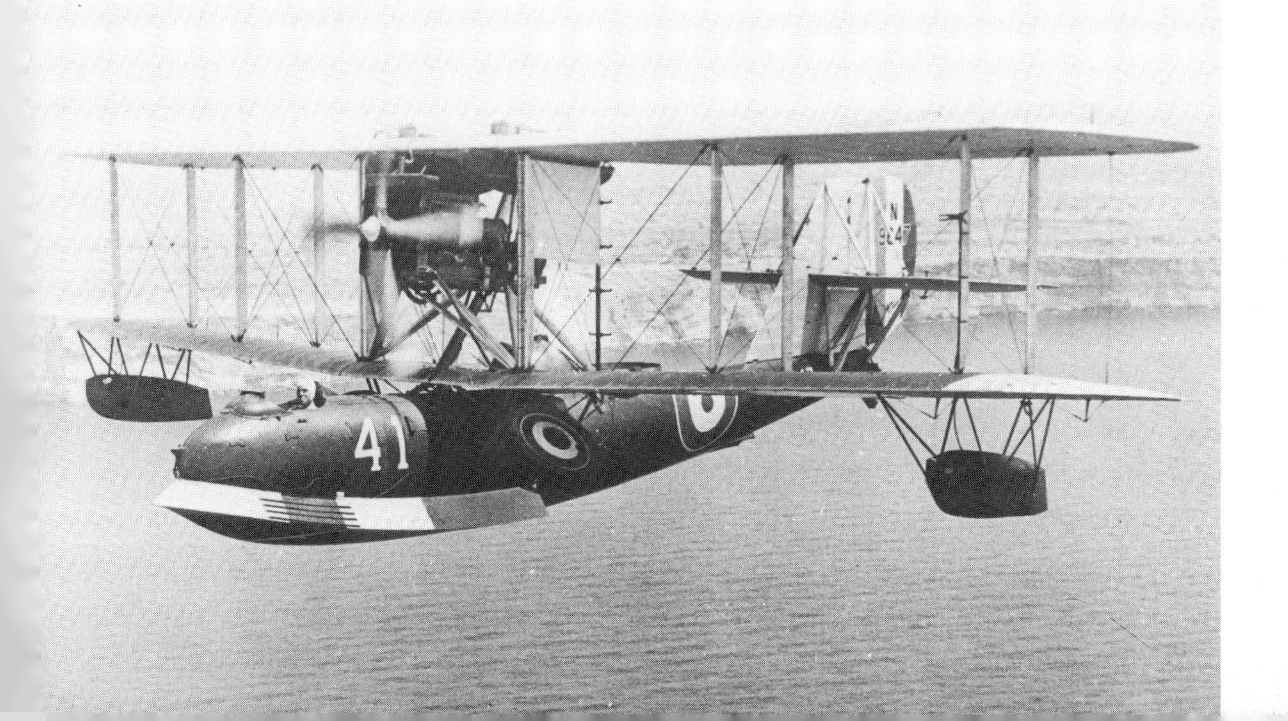

▲9

▲10 ▼11

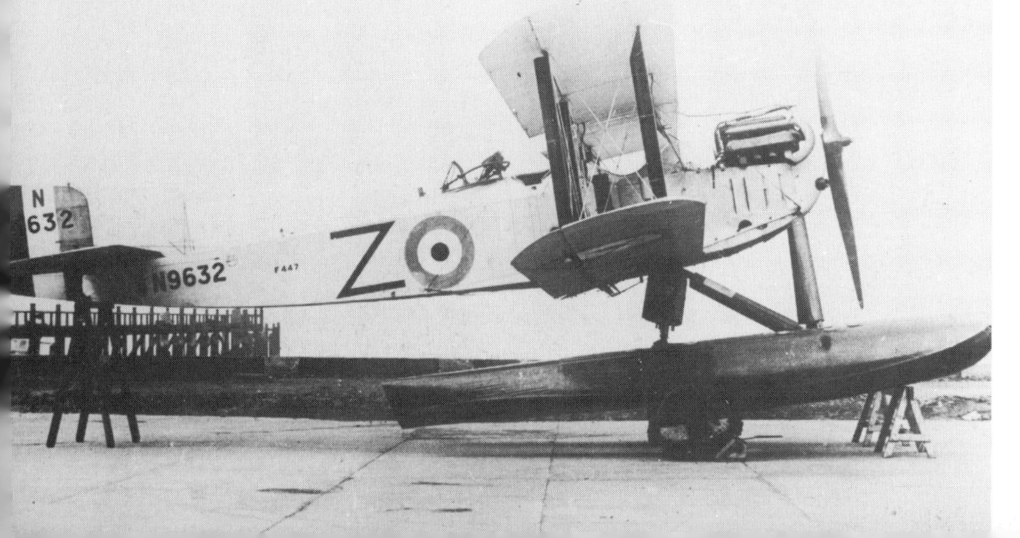

9. The ungainly lines of the Avro Bison are clearly seen in this photograph of, probably a Mk. I of No. 423 (Fleet Spotter) Flight. The observer and wireless operator gained access by mean of a ladder on the port side to th gun turret on top of the fuselage from which they descended into a large, well-equipped cabin wit two generous windows.

10. Lined up in 1924, probably at Leuchars, are aircraft and me from HMS *Eagle*. On the left ar a Blackburn Blackburn I of No. 422 Flight and the Blackburn Darts of No. 460 Flight bearing white fleet numbers on the blac rectangle associated with that carrier. On the right are the Flycatchers of No. 402 Flight, at this stage not yet painted with black squares and therefore bearing their fleet number in black; at the far end of this line are two more Blackburns.

11. Fairey IIID Mk. I seaplane N9632 'Z' was delivered from t maker's Hamble factory to the RAF Unit in the seaplane carri HMS *Pegasus* on 25 January 1924 to participate in a Far Eastern photographic survey expedition. The ship sailed for Singapore with this and five other IIIDs on 21 March 1924 eventually returning to Plymouth on 31 March 1925. (Via J. D. Oughton)

12▲

12. A waterline view of HMS *Hermes* whilst at anchor off Malta in 1924, when the ship was attached to the Mediterranean Fleet. The exaggerated flare of the forward flight deck was designed to provide the greatest possible width for take-off. The superstructure – offset to starboard as an 'island' – was the first of its kind for a British carrier, but its size created problems. The ship, the first ever to be designed from the start as an aircraft carrier, was quite small by the standards of later post-war carriers. (Via W. A. Woodall)

13▲ 14▼

13. Blackburn Dart N9550 of No. 460 (Fleet Torpedo) Flight, seen here dropping a torpedo off the coast of Malta on 12 January 1925, has its nose painted black and carries the white fleet number '62' on the black rectangle of HMS *Eagle*. (FAA Museum)

14. A batch of 36 Westland Walruses was produced in 1921–22, the prototype modification (J6585), developed from the DH9A, having been built by Armstrong-Whitworth and given the unlikely name Tadpole. N9512 of No. 420 (Fleet Spotter) Flight, from HMS *Furious*, is seen here on 23 June 1924, after its undercarriage broke while flying from Christchurch and it had to force-land in Weymouth Bay.

▲15 ▼16

15. Fairey IIID Mk. II S1019, of No. 440 (Fleet Reconnaissance) Flight, piloted by Captain G. E. Wildman-Lushington RM, flying over the Mediterranean off the coast of Malta, probably in early 1926. The white fleet number '40' is carried on the black rectangle of HMS *Eagle*. The undercarriage components were painted black, the wheel discs being white. (Via Owen Cathcart-Jones)

16. The seaplane carrier HMS *Vindictive*, at anchor at Wei-hai-Wei in Northern China in 1926, hoists out N9469, one of the six Fairey IIIDs of No. 444 (Fleet Reconnaissance) Flight carried by the ship between 1925 and 1929. (Via W. A. Woodall)

17. Avro Bison II N9977, of No. 421A (Fleet Spotter) Flight, flying in home waters around 1926, bears the fleet number '34' in white on the diagonal red band of HMS *Furious*. The pilot was situated at such a height that it was necessary to have a fixed ladder extending from the lower starboard wing root to just forward of his cockpit. (RAF Museum)

18. Flight Lieutenant Gerald Boyce's Blackburn Dart, N9804 of No. 462 (Fleet Torpedo) Flight, making the first night-time carrier deck landing on HMS *Furious* on 6 May 1926. The fleet number '74' is carried in white on a red fuselage band, and the wheel discs bear a black swastika. (G. S. Leslie/J. M. Bruce collection)

19. Fairey Flycatcher N9962, of No. 404B (Fleet Fighter) Flight from HMS *Argus*, flying over Hong Kong Island around 1927. Shore-based at Kai Tak, the aircraft carried no fleet number at that stage. The large spinner fitted to the early machines was later abandoned.

17▲

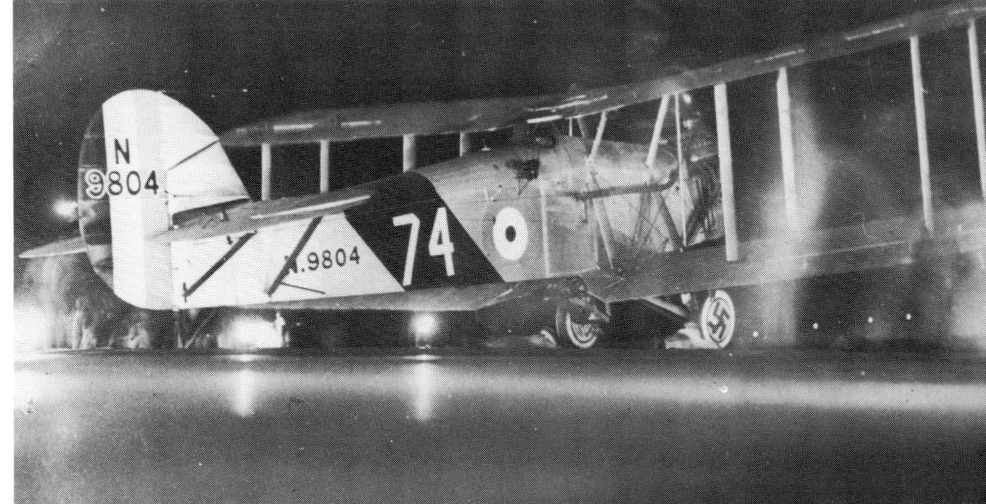

18▲ **19▼**

▲20

20. The pilot of Fairey IIID N9770, of No. 421 (Fleet Spotter) Flight, poses by his aircraft on Kiangnan racecourse, Shanghai, during the 1927 troubles. Fleet Air Arm machines operated from an improvised 400-yard strip parallel to the grandstand, carrying out patrols around the Settlement, which became surrounded by rebel troops. The aircraft bears the white fleet number '53' on the green rectangle of HMS *Argus*. (FAA Museum)

21. Fairey Flycatcher N9908 '2', of No. 403 (Fleet Fighter) Flight from HMS *Hermes*, after coming to grief in Hong Kong harbour around 1927. This unit had an individual approach to the application of fuselage markings at that time, white diamonds, chevrons and other shapes being employed as backgrounds to fleet numbers instead of the more normal vertical or diagonal bands. (RAF Museum P.8387)

▼21

22▲

22. Fairey IIID floatplanes (including S1008, S1028 and S1091) and personnel of No. 422 (Fleet Spotter) Flight ashore from HMS *Argus* at Wei-hai-Wei around July 1927.

23▲ 24▼

23. HMS *Furious* in 1927, with her outboard palisades and hinged wireless masts all raised. The palisades had only recently been fitted and proved a great success in preventing wayward aircraft from going overboard. In an extensive refit at Devonport in 1930–31, the forward end of the flight deck was stepped up when the quarterdeck was raised. A centrally placed, retractable auxiliary charthouse is seen in the raised position at the forward end of the flight deck. In a later refit in 1938–39, a small island was fitted at the starboard edge of the flight deck. (RAF Museum P.014554)

24. Fairey IIID N9770 temporarily fitted with twin wooden floats whilst with No. 441 (Fleet Reconnaissance) Flight around 1927-28. It carries the white fleet number '53'in the green rectangle of HMS *Argus*, then serving on the China Station. (FAA Museum)

▲25

▲26 ▼27

25. A Fairey Flycatcher of No. 404A (Fleet Fighter) Flight on the lower flying-off deck of HMS *Furious* around 1927. The lateral protective windscreen on this deck is in the 'up' position, but its counterpart on the upper flight deck is lowered, as are the hinged wireless masts. The 'T' markings on the latter formed part of a visual signal to the carrier's aircraft. (FAA Museum)

26. Fairey IIIF Mk II S1211, of No. 445 (Fleet Reconnaissance) Flight, possibly at Hal Far around 1928. This early version had an angular stepped fin and rudder, replaced on later marks by a more pleasing, elongated, curved design. The fleet number '41' is carried on the light blue diagonal fuselage band of HMS *Courageous*. Flight markings comprised red and white fin checks, and blue wheel discs with a silver star. The upper decking is painted black to counteract glare. (Via Tim Hills)

27. Blackburn Dart N9815, of No. 464 (Fleet Torpedo) Flight, after landing aboard HMS *Courageous* on 29 June 1928 during exercises off Malta. The wing-grabbing party dashes forward as the aircraft comes to a halt after making an emergency landing with torpedo up and failing oil pressure. The aircraft had bounced after hitting the round-down, the undercarriage being strained and the port wheel torn off. The aircraft carries white fleet number '72' on a diagonal light blue fuselage band, and the fin bears diagonal black and white stripes. (Via D. Thompson)

28. The Blackburn Darts of No. 461 (Fleet Torpedo) Flight flying past the erected palisades of HMS *Furious* around 1928–29. These aircraft carried their full fleet numbers in the range 60 to 65 on the fins, with only the last digit repeated on the red fuselage bands. Palisades were hinged metal and rope constructions extending from each side of the flight deck to catch aircraft in danger of going over the side while landing on. (FAA Museum)

28▲

29. Fitted with metal floats, Fairey IIIF Mk II S1255, of No. 440 (Fleet Reconnaissance) Flight from HMS *Hermes*, is at rest on the water, probably at Hong Kong around 1929. The black fleet number '45' is carried on a broad white band which tapers to a point at the top of the fuselage. (Via Tim Hills)

29▼

▲30

30. The battlecruiser HMS *Hood*, sunk by the German pocket battleship *Bismarck* in May 1941, is seen here with a Fairey Flycatcher mounted on a wooden ramp on 'B' turret in the late 1920s. This method of launching landplanes from warships was a relic of the First World War and was not superseded until the installation of catapults in the early 1930s. (Via Ian Huntley)

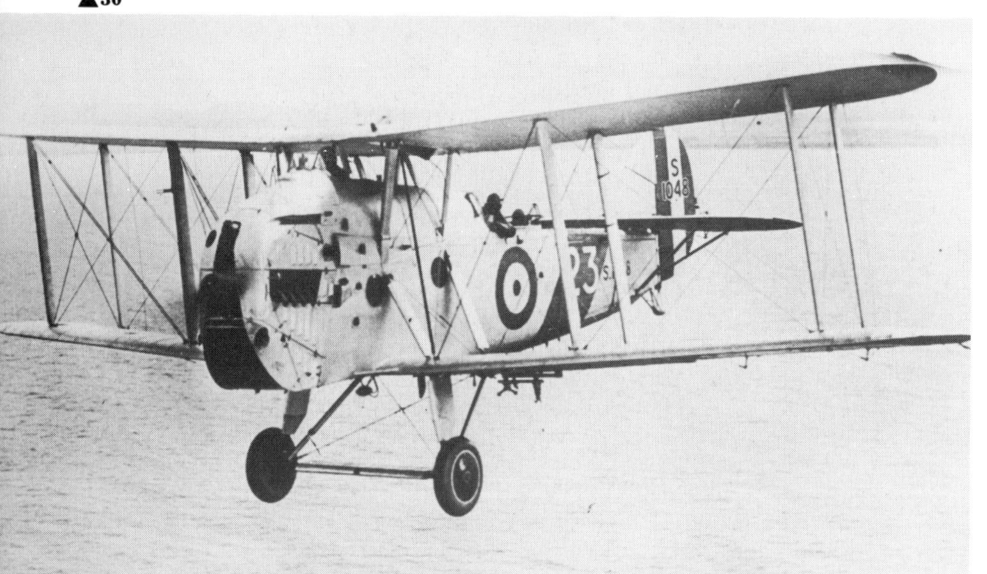

▲31 ▼32

31. Blackburn Blackburn II S1048, of No. 449 (Fleet Spotter Reconnaissance) Flight, HMS *Furious*, around 1929. The aircraft carries the white fleet number '23' on a diagonal red band. The ugly lines at the front of the Blackburn, necessitated by the provision of a large cabin for the crew, are clearly seen. In this later version all the fuel tanks were carried internally, and the pilot's vision was improved by leaving a gap between the top of the fuselage and the upper mainplanes.

32. The Fairey Flycatcher (S1278) of Lieutenant-Commander E. M. C. Abel Smith the Commanding Officer of No. 406 (Fleet Fighter) Flight from HMS *Glorious*, seen at Hal Far, Malta, on the morning of 22 August 1930, following a landin accident the previous night. Thi aircraft was used for camera gu practice, the gun being visible here on the lower starboard mainplane. The black fleet number '7' is carried on a yello diagonal band edged in white, the wheel discs being similarly coloured. (FAA Museum)

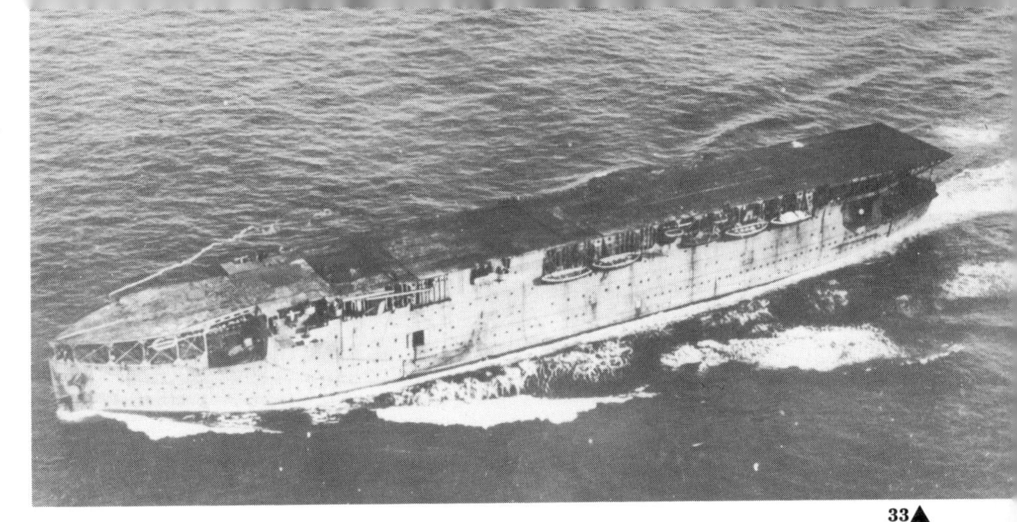

33▲

33. HMS *Argus* as viewed from 700 feet by the crew of one of her aircraft on 23 January 1930. Commissioned in September 1918, this ship was later to see operational service for a time in the Second World War before being relegated to deck landing training duties. (RAF Museum P.10281)

34▲ 35▼

34. A Fairey Flycatcher of No. 408 (Fleet Fighter) Flight emerging from the hangar and preparing to take off from the rather wet lower flying deck of HMS *Glorious*. On the nose, just forward of the machine-gun, can be seen a reproduction of the ship's badge consisting of a gold rose with a silver centre on a red background. The lowered protective windscreen can be seen in the foreground. (RAF Museum P.012730)

35. A smokescreen of stannic chloride being laid in Scapa Flow by a Fairey IIIF of the Fleet Air Arm in 1930. Such trials were carried out periodically, and proved of value during the Second World War when Fairey Swordfish laid a smokescreen over the English Channel during the Normandy invasion to hide the movements of British and American ships. (P. H. Plater via B. Goulding)

36. This photograph of Fairey Flycatcher N9928 illustrates a short-lived attempt at using fuselage pennants instead of bands. Here Lieutenant-Commander J. F. M. Robertson is flying an aircraft of No. 401 (Fleet Fighter) Flight in late 1930. It has a striped light blue pennant on the upper decking of the fuselage, and a design of the same colour on the wheel discs. (RAF Museum 5015-3)

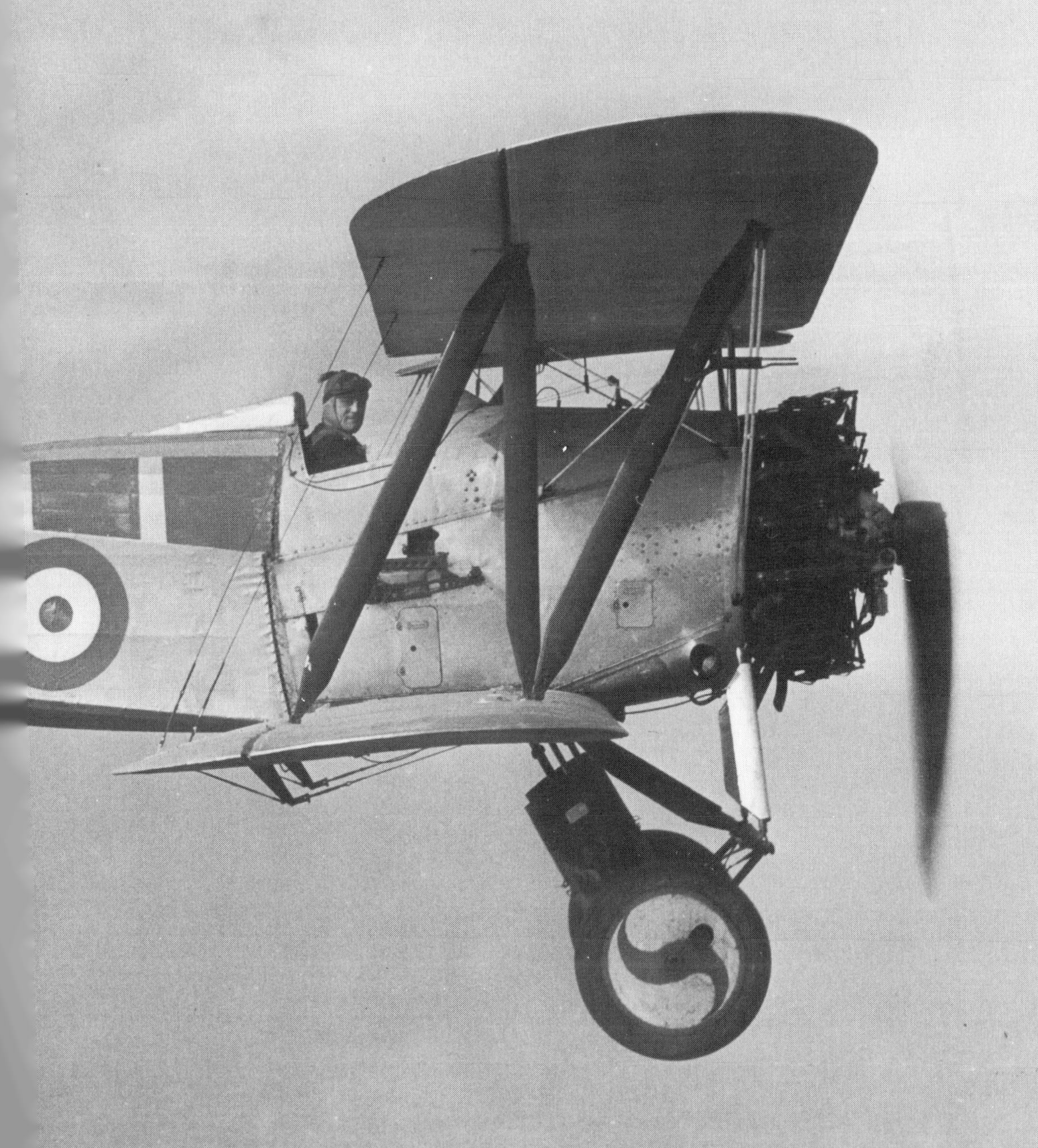

▲37

▲38 ▼39

37. In September 1930 HMS *Eagle* carried out a cruise in the eastern Mediterranean. She arrived at Alexandria on 30 September, and all her aircraft flew ashore to Aboukir. In addition to the Flycatchers of No. 402 (Fleet Fighter) Flight and the Darts of No. 460 (Fleet Torpedo Bomber) Flight, some of which are seen here, are also carried the Fairey IIIFs of No. 448 (Fleet Spotter Reconnaissance) Flight. On 11 October 1930 the aircraft re-embarked and the ship sailed north for Athens. (FAA Museum)

38. Around 1930 various new prototype fighters were tested by No. 405 (Fleet Fighter) Flight, including trials aboard HMS *Furious*. In addition to Blackburn Nautilus N234, which bore the red fleet number '18' on a diagonal red band outlined in white, tests were also undertaken with the Fairey Fleetwing, Armstrong-Whitworth Starling, Hawker Naval Hart and Hawker Hornet. None of these was ordered as a replacement for the ubiquitous Flycatcher, but the last two types were developed into the successful Osprey and Nimrod. (Via J. D. Oughton)

39. Very few De Havilland DH9As saw service with the Fleet Air Arm but J8482, seen here, was used in 1930 to test the safety nets, or palisades, aboard HMS *Glorious*. The aircraft still bears the code number '2' on its nose from previous service with No. 35 Squadron, RAF Bircham Newton. J8143 '4', from the same squadron, carried out similar trials aboard HMS *Eagle*. (Sqn Ldr J. Burnet, via FAA Museum)

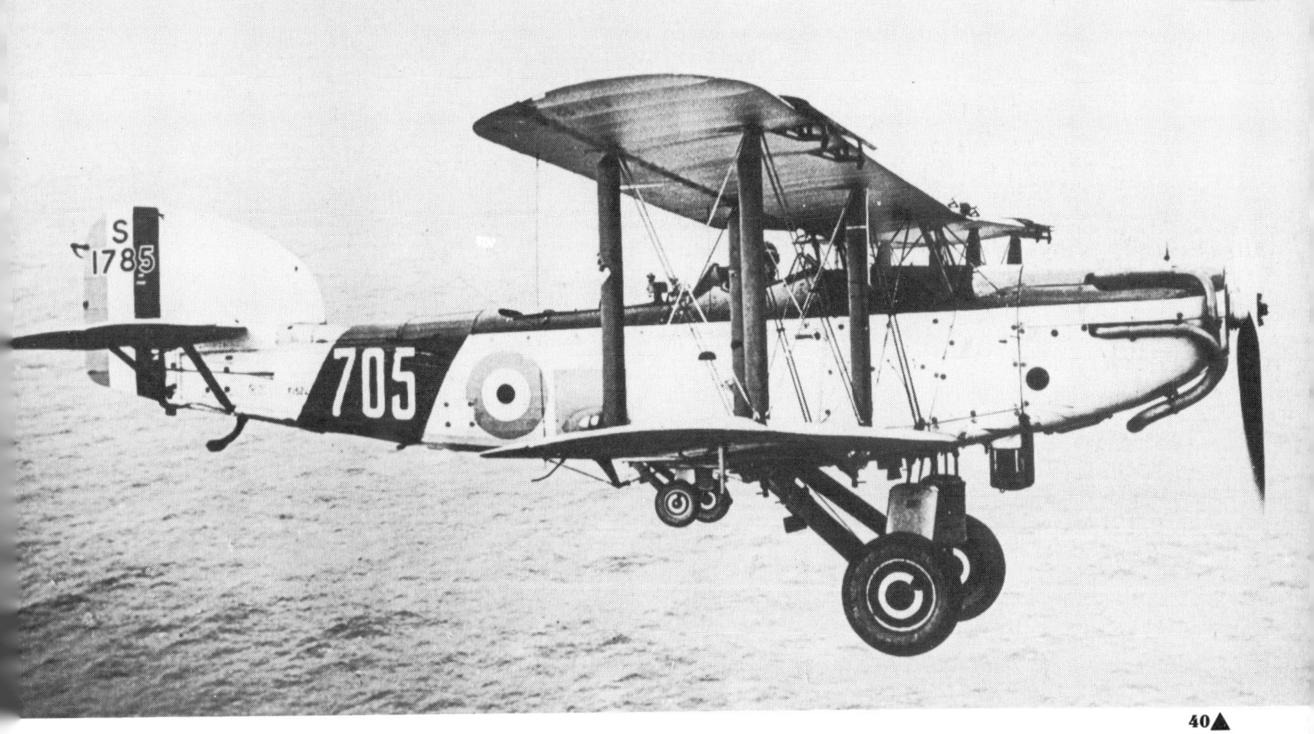

40▲

40. Fairey IIIF Mk IIIB S1785 '705', of No. 822 (Spotter Reconnaissance) Squadron from HMS *Furious* and piloted by Flying Officer R. A. McMurtrie, in 1933. Despite appearances, the aircraft has not sprouted an extra pair of miniature wheels; these belong to an accompanying aircraft. The small windsock-type pennant in the top right of the photograph is attached to the port wing of the photographing aircraft. (Gp Capt R. A. McMurtrie)

41. Fairey IIIFs of No. 443 (Fleet Spotter Reconnaissance) Flight from HMS *Furious*, temporarily fitted with metal floats and based at Portland, around May 1930. Half a century later this area has become more familiar with ships' helicopters. (Via W. A. Woodall)

41▼

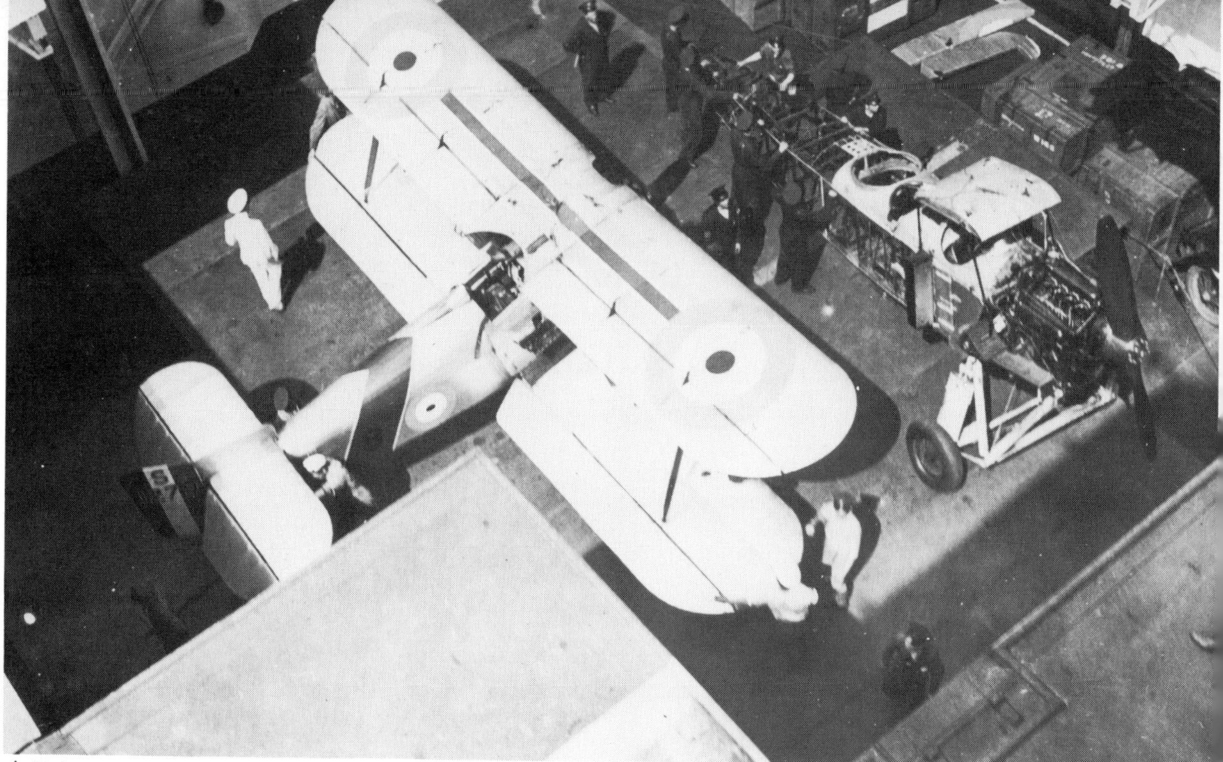

▲42

42. Fairey Flycatcher S1279 of No. 408 (Fleet Fighter) Flight being brought up from the hangar deck of HMS *Glorious* on the lift (which is 'T' shaped to accommodate the aircraft's wings). The fleet number '8' is carried on a yellow fuselage band outlined in white, the band between the wing roundels being of the same colours. The photograph was taken about 1931. (FAA Museum)

43. Turret platforms were a legacy from the First World War. They continued throughout the 1920s, only being overtaken in the early 1930s when the science of catapulting became sufficiently developed. In this instance Fairey Flycatcher S12921 '3', of No. 406 (Fleet Fighter) Flight, is departing from a wooden platform mounted above 'B' turret of an 'R' Class battleship around 1931, while the ship steams into wind. (FAA Museum)

▼43

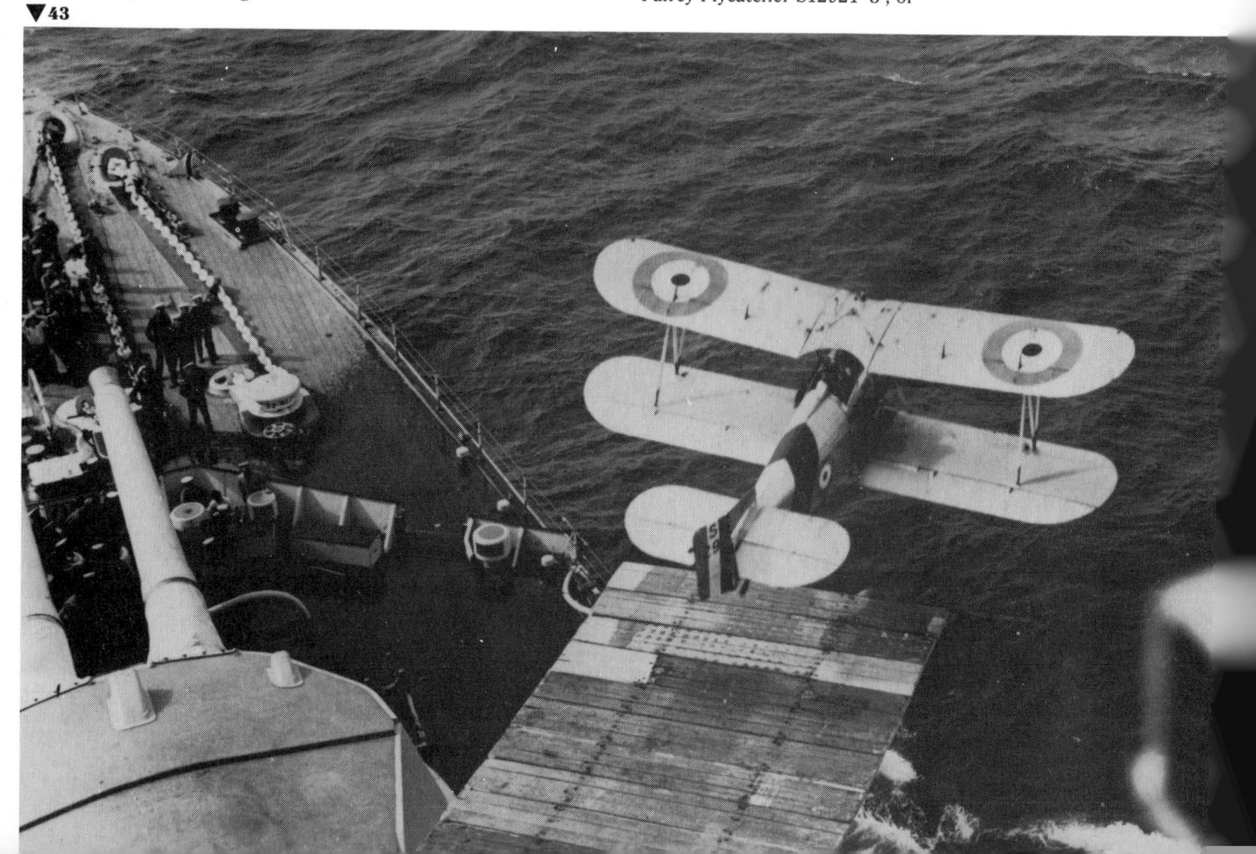

FLEET AIR ARM UNITS

No.	Period	Aircraft	Ships
401	April 1923–April 1933	Nightjar, Flycatcher, Nimrod	*Hermes, Vindictive, Courageous, Furious*
402	April 1923–April 1933	Flycatcher, Nimrod	*Eagle, Courageous*
403	June 1923–July 1936	Nightjar, Plover, Flycatcher, Osprey, Walrus	*Hermes*, 5th Cruiser Sqn
404	July 1923–April 1933	Nightjar, Plover, Nimrod, Osprey	*Furious, Argus, Courageous*
405	May 1924–April 1933	Flycatcher, Osprey	*Furious, Glorious*, 5th Cruiser Sqn
406	May 1924–July 1936	Flycatcher, Osprey, IIIF	*Glorious, Furious*, 4th Cruiser Sqn
407	Sept. 1927–July 1936	Flycatcher, Osprey, Walrus	*Courageous, Furious*, 2nd Cruiser Sqn
408	March 1929–April 1933	Flycatcher, Nimrod, Osprey	*Glorious*

leet Spotter Flights

No.	Period	Aircraft	Ships
420	April 1923–April 1929	Walrus, Blackburn	*Furious*
421	April 1923–April 1929	Walrus, Bison, IIIF	*Furious, Eagle*
422	April 1923–April 1929	Walrus, Blackburn, IIID	*Eagle, Argus*
423	Nov. 1923–July 1924	Walrus, Bison, IIIF	*Argus, Hermes, Eagle*

leet Reconnaissance Flights

No.	Period	Aircraft	Ships
40	May 1923–June 1933	Seagull, IIID, IIIF	*Eagle, Hermes*
41	April 1923–April 1933	Panther, IIID, IIIF	*Hermes, Eagle, Argus, Glorious*
42	April 1923–April 1933	Panther, IIID, IIIF	*Argus, Hermes, Furious*
43	May 1923–July 1936	IIID, IIIF, Osprey	*Furious, Argus*, 2nd Cruiser Sqn, 6th/8th Cruiser Sqn
44	Jan. 1925–July 1936	IIID, IIIF, Seal, Walrus, Osprey, Shark, Swordfish	*Vindictive*, 2nd Battle Sqn & Battle Cruiser Sqn, 1st Battle Sqn & 1st Cruiser Sqn
45	Sept. 27–July 1936	IIID, IIIF, Osprey	*Courageous*, 3rd Cruiser Sqn
46	Sept. 1927–April 1933	IIIF	*Courageous*
47	April 1929–July 1936	IIIF, Osprey	*Furious, Glorious*, 1st Cruiser Sqn, 1st Battle Sqn
8	April 1929–April 1933	IIIF	*Eagle, Glorious*
9	April 1929–April 1933	Blackburn, IIIF	*Furious, Courageous*
0	April 1929–April 1933	Blackburn, IIIF	*Argus, Courageous*

et Torpedo Flights

No.	Period	Aircraft	Ships
0	April 1923–April 1933	Dart, Ripon, IIIF	*Eagle, Glorious*
461	April 1923–April 1933	Walrus, Dart, Ripon	*Furious, Glorious*
462	July 1924–April 1933	Dart, Ripon	*Furious, Glorious*
463	Sept. 1927–April 1933	Dart	*Courageous*
464	Sept. 1927–April 1933	Dart	*Courageous*
465	March 1932–April 1933	Ripon	*Furious*
466	March 1932–April 1933	Ripon	*Furious*

Catapult Flights/Squadrons

No.	Period	Aircraft	Ships
701	July 1936–Sept. 1939	IIIF, Osprey, Shark, Seal, Swordfish	1st Battle Sqn
702	July 1936–Sept. 1939	Seal, Walrus	2nd Battle Sqn
705	July 1936–Sept. 1939	Shark, Swordfish	Battle Cruiser Sqn
711	July 1936–Sept. 1939	Osprey, Walrus	1st Cruiser Sqn
712	July 1936–Sept. 1939	Osprey, Walrus	2nd Cruiser Sqn
713	July 1936–Sept. 1939	Osprey, Seafox	3rd Cruiser Sqn
714	July 1936–Sept. 1939	IIIF, Osprey, Seafox, Walrus	4th Cruiser Sqn
715	July 1936–Sept. 1939	Osprey, Walrus	5th Cruiser Sqn
716	July 1936–Sept. 1939	Osprey, Seafox	6th Cruiser Sqn
718	July 1936–Sept. 1939	IIIF, Osprey, Walrus, Seafox	8th Cruiser Sqn
720	July 1936–Sept. 1939	Walrus	New Zealand Division

Fleet Fighter Squadrons

No.	Period	Aircraft	Ships
800	April 1933–Sept. 1939	Osprey, Nimrod	*Courageous, Ark Royal*
801	April 1933–Sept. 1939	Flycatcher, Nimrod, Osprey	*Furious, Courageous*
802	April 1933–Sept. 1939	Nimrod, Osprey	*Glorious*
803	April 1933–April 1937	Osprey	*Eagle, Hermes*
	Nov. 1938–Sept. 1939	Osprey, Nimrod, Skua	*Ark Royal*

Torpedo Bomber (later Torpedo Spotter Reconnaissance) Squadrons

No.	Period	Aircraft	Ships
810	April 1933–Sept. 1939	Dart, Ripon, Baffin, Shark, Swordfish	*Courageous, Ark Royal*
811	April 1933–Sept. 1939	Ripon, Baffin, Swordfish	*Furious, Courageous*
812	April 1933–Sept. 1939	Ripon, Baffin, Swordfish	*Glorious, Furious*
813	Jan. 1937–April 1939	Swordfish	*Eagle*

COLOURS 1920–39

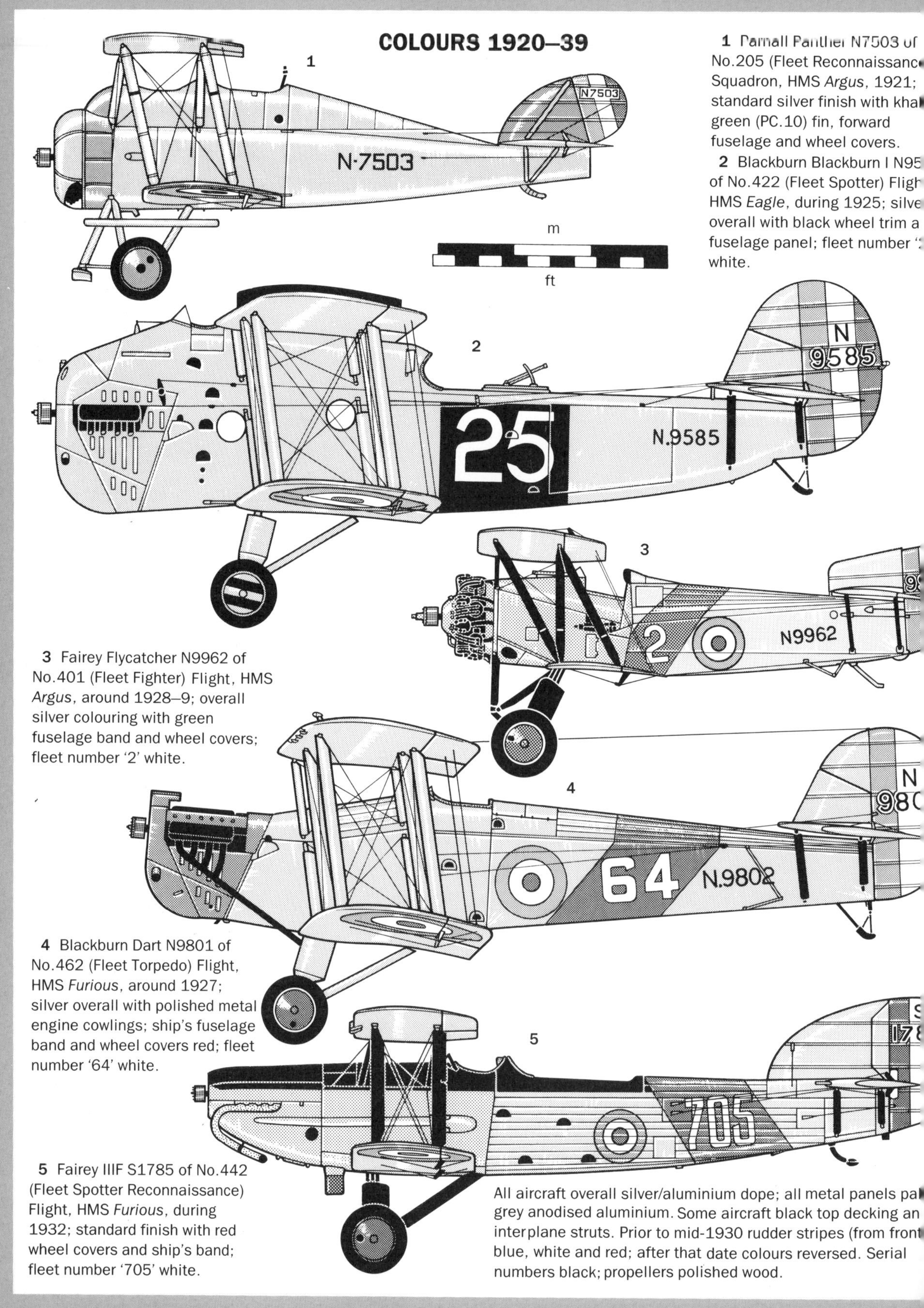

1 Parnall Panther N7503 of No.205 (Fleet Reconnaissance Squadron, HMS *Argus*, 1921; standard silver finish with kha green (PC.10) fin, forward fuselage and wheel covers.

2 Blackburn Blackburn I N95 of No.422 (Fleet Spotter) Fligh HMS *Eagle*, during 1925; silve overall with black wheel trim a fuselage panel; fleet number ' white.

3 Fairey Flycatcher N9962 of No.401 (Fleet Fighter) Flight, HMS *Argus*, around 1928–9; overall silver colouring with green fuselage band and wheel covers; fleet number '2' white.

4 Blackburn Dart N9801 of No.462 (Fleet Torpedo) Flight, HMS *Furious*, around 1927; silver overall with polished metal engine cowlings; ship's fuselage band and wheel covers red; fleet number '64' white.

5 Fairey IIIF S1785 of No.442 (Fleet Spotter Reconnaissance) Flight, HMS *Furious*, during 1932; standard finish with red wheel covers and ship's band; fleet number '705' white.

All aircraft overall silver/aluminium dope; all metal panels pa grey anodised aluminium. Some aircraft black top decking an interplane struts. Prior to mid-1930 rudder stripes (from front blue, white and red; after that date colours reversed. Serial numbers black; propellers polished wood.

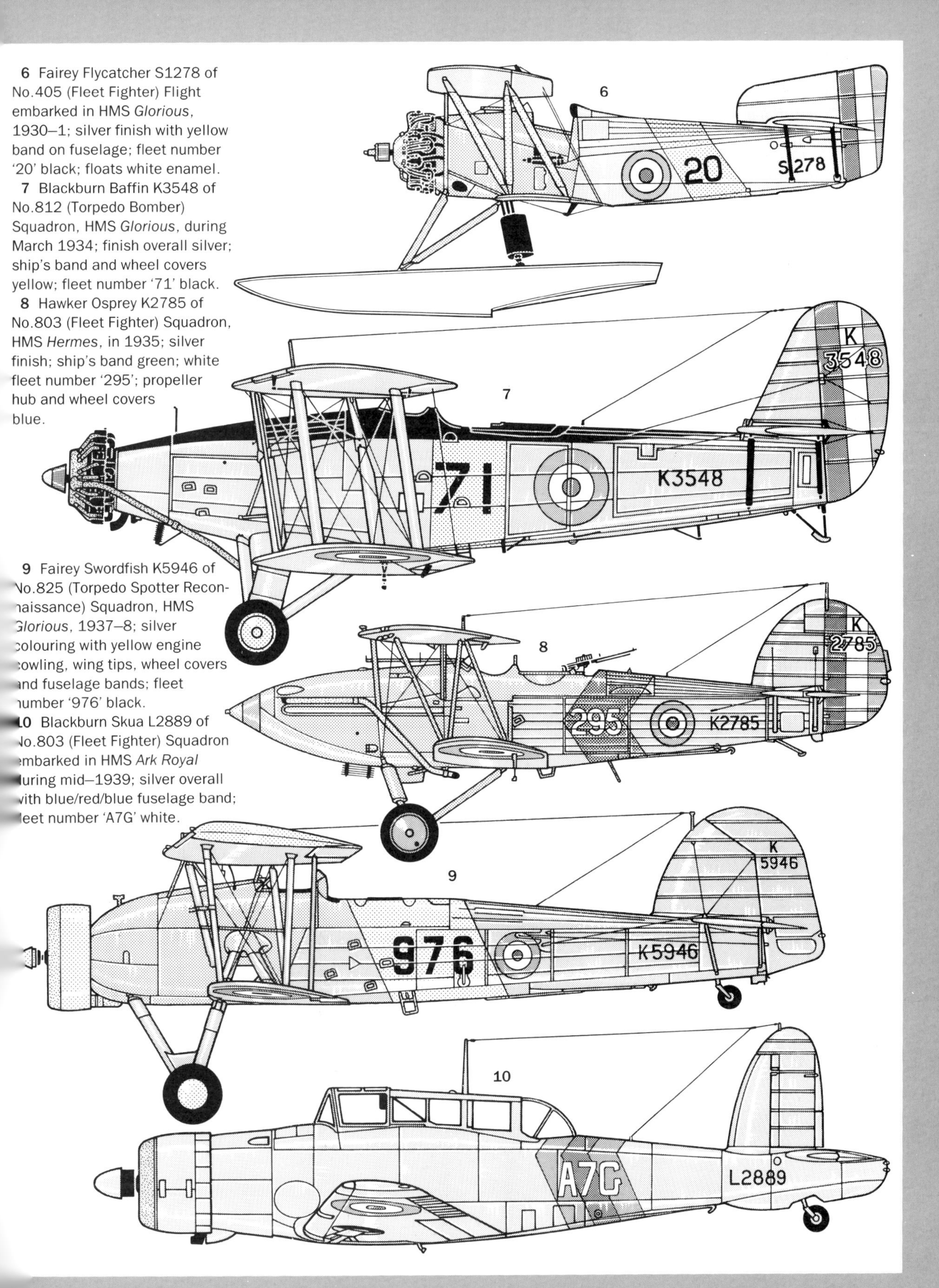

6 Fairey Flycatcher S1278 of No.405 (Fleet Fighter) Flight embarked in HMS *Glorious*, 1930–1; silver finish with yellow band on fuselage; fleet number '20' black; floats white enamel.

7 Blackburn Baffin K3548 of No.812 (Torpedo Bomber) Squadron, HMS *Glorious*, during March 1934; finish overall silver; ship's band and wheel covers yellow; fleet number '71' black.

8 Hawker Osprey K2785 of No.803 (Fleet Fighter) Squadron, HMS *Hermes*, in 1935; silver finish; ship's band green; white fleet number '295'; propeller hub and wheel covers blue.

9 Fairey Swordfish K5946 of No.825 (Torpedo Spotter Reconnaissance) Squadron, HMS *Glorious*, 1937–8; silver colouring with yellow engine cowling, wing tips, wheel covers and fuselage bands; fleet number '976' black.

10 Blackburn Skua L2889 of No.803 (Fleet Fighter) Squadron embarked in HMS *Ark Royal* during mid–1939; silver overall with blue/red/blue fuselage band; fleet number 'A7G' white.

No.	Period	Aircraft	Ships
814	Nov. 1938–April 1939	Swordfish	*Ark Royal*

Spotter Reconnaissance (later Torpedo Spotter Reconnaissance) Squadrons

No.	Period	Aircraft	Ships
820	April 1933–Sept. 1939	IIIF, Seal, Baffin, Shark, Swordfish	*Courageous, Ark Royal*
821	April 1933–Sept. 1939	IIIF, Seal, Shark, Swordfish	*Courageous, Ark Royal*
822	April 1933–Sept. 1939	IIIF, Seal, Shark, Swordfish	*Courageous, Furious*
823	April 1933–Sept. 1939	IIIF, Seal, Swordfish	*Glorious, Courageous*
824	April 1933–Oct. 1934	IIIF	*Eagle*
	Oct. 1934–Sept. 1939	Seal, Swordfish	*Hermes, Eagle*
825	Oct. 1934–Sept. 1939	IIIF, Swordfish	*Eagle, Glorious*

COLOUR SCHEMES

For most of the period covered, the general finish of Fleet Air Arm aircraft was overall silver with black or natural metal engine cowlings. To avoid dazzle, the upper fuselage decking was either black or very dark grey.

RAF-style red, white and blue roundels were generally carried either side of the fuselage, above the upper mainplanes and below the lower mainplanes. Rudder stripe colours (reading from the front) were blue, white and red until mid-1930, after which they were reversed.

Carrier identity colours were introduced around 1924–5 to be used on the fuselage bands of every aircraft flown from a particular carrier. Colour allocations were as follows:

HMS *Argus* green (until 1930)
HMS *Ark Royal* blue/red/blue stripes
HMS *Eagle* black
HMS *Courageous* light blue
HMS *Furious* red
HMS *Glorious* yellow
HMS *Hermes* white until 1933, then green from 1934

Each individual aircraft was allocated a fleet number, which in effect was a code number. It initially comprised one or two digits carried either side of the fuselage, and occasionally on the upper and lower wing surfaces. On the fuselage sides, the fleet number was normally carried on the coloured carrier band, usually in black or white. The carrier band could be painted either in front of or behind the roundel, the latter being sometimes omitted altogether if space were limited. Catapult aircraft carried no coloured bands, numbers being usually painted in black straight on to the fuselage sides. In 1932 a revised system of fleet numbers was introduced, in which up to three digits could be used. In some instances individual, flight or squadron colours were painted across the upper wing surfaces, between the roundels. Occasionally the fleet number, or its last digit, would be reproduced on the inner or centre upper-wing sections in the form of the equivalent naval flags.

In May 1939 fleet numbers were replaced by letter/number/letter codes, in which the first two components identified the squadron concerned and the last letter gave the individual identity of that particular aircraft. These were similar in appearance to RAF codes, but the method of applying them was somewhat different, and they should therefore always be read from left to right, irrespective of the location of the fuselage roundel (if carried). Such codes were initially painted on the peacetime silver finish, but shortly before the outbreak of war this finish was replaced by camouflage.

 44

45▲

4. Acting as a station flight and ɛet requirements unit, the RAF ase Miscellaneous Flight erated four Fairey IIIFs from l Far around 1931. S1457 rried its identification number on a slender vertical fuselage nd, and a Maltese cross was inted on the fin; it is here accompanied by another aircraft of the flight, only the wheels of which can be seen. (FAA Museum)

45. The battleship HMS *Valiant* at anchor during the Home Fleet Spring Cruise in March 1931. Fairey IIIF Mk III S1484 '98', of No. 443 (Fleet Spotter Reconnaissance) Flight, is being hoisted over the stern catapult. Shortly afterwards this aircraft was transferred to the cruiser HMS *York* and its fleet number was then changed to '57'. (RAF Museum P.101110)

46. The Fleet Air Arm operated a few Avro 504 trainers, mainly shore-based at Gosport and Leuchars. This 504N (K1813), which was flown by 'A' Flight, RAF Base Gosport, is here seen aboard a carrier, probably about to take off. The ship's palisades are in the 'up' position.

46▼

▲47 ▼48

47. A not unusual end for a prewar Fleet Air Arm aircraft: crew of the ship's whaler help retrieve Fairey Flycatcher '15' No. 407 (Fleet Fighter) Flight from HMS *Courageous*, pilote by Flight Lieutenant W. Sand son AFC, the Commanding Officer, after it has come to a sticky end, probably off Malta around 1931. (Via D. Thompson)

48. Fairey Flycatcher S1297, fitted with metal floats, leavi the catapult of a battleship in coastal waters. On the centre section of the upper wing car seen straps for hoisting the aircraft back on board ship a it returns to land alongside. (Ransomes & Rapier Ltd)

49▲ 50▼

9. Blackburn Ripon II S1564 of
o. 466 (Fleet Torpedo Bomber)
light, HMS *Furious*, around
932. The white fleet number
3' is carried on a red chevron,
e wheel discs also being red.
n the fin can be seen the flight's
official bird badge. (Official)

. Fairey Flycatchers of No. 407
leet Fighter) Flight in loose
rmation over HMS *Courageous*
ring the 1932 Spring Cruise.
AF Museum P.10274)

▲51 ▼52

51. Fairey Flycatcher S1274 of No. 401 (Fleet Fighter) Flight taking off around 1932–33 from the lower foredeck of HMS *Furious*, with spray streaming over the bow of the ship. The fleet number '527' is carried on a red diagonal fuselage band and the fin is black with a diagonal red band edged in white and carrying the unofficial flight crest. In the background, HMS *Courageous* is seen in company. (Via Gp Capt. R. A. McMurtrie)

52. Fairey IIIF Mk III S1355 of the Seaplane Training Flight taxies towards the Calshot slipway around 1932. The ground crew stands ready to pull her in. (Gp Capt. R. A. McMurtrie)

53. A Fairey IIIF comes in to land aboard HMS *Furious* while the wing-grabbing party stands poised to dash forward and secure her. (Gp Capt. R. A. McMurtrie)

54. A busy scene on the flight deck of HMS *Courageous* around 1932–33. In the foreground, Fairey IIIF Mk III S1321 '724', of No. 445 (Fleet Spotter Reconnaissance) Flight, is held by the wings before starting its take-off run, whilst further IIIFs of Nos. 445 and 450 (FSR) Flights are ranged to follow on. Palisades are raised at the side of the ship and two rescue destroyers stand by. (Via D. Thompson)

55. Officers and men of HMS *Courageous* watch Fairey IIIF S1211 '748', of No. 450 (Fleet Spotter Reconnaissance) Flight, take off above the lowered protective windscreen with the assistance of the ship's steam accelerator, or catapult, around 1932–33. (Via D. Thompson)

53▲

54▲ 55▼

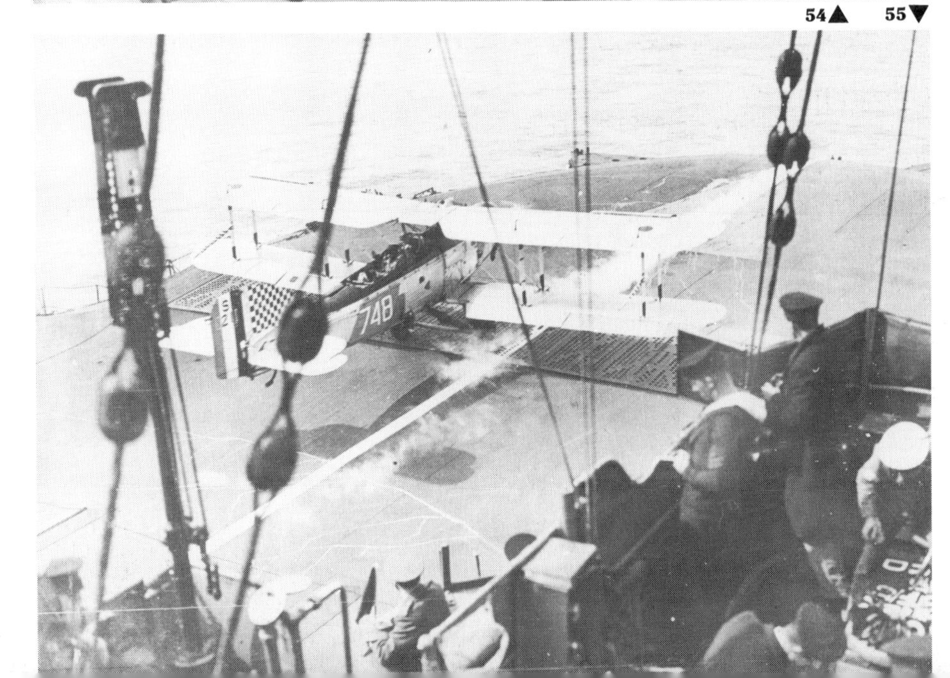

▲**56**

56. This pleasing close-up photograph of a Fairey Flycatcher of No. 800 (Fleet Fighter) Squadron from HMS *Courageous* shows clearly one of the two side-mounted Vickers machine-guns. The fleet number is unclear but is probably '509', the marking under the inboard area of the lower port wing being therefore a red and white No. 9 naval flag. The black fin carries an unofficial gold crest comprising the squadron number superimposed on two crossed swords and a trident, later redesigned and approved as the new-style official crest. (Via J. D. Oughton)

▼**57**

57. Another of the potential new fleet fighters tested aboard HMS *Furious* by No. 405 (Fleet Fighter) Flight in about 1930: Fairey Fleetwing N235 carries the fleet number '19' on a red diagonal band edged in white. (Capt. M. Farquhar)

58. Fairey IIIF Mk III S1487 '86' of the newly formed No. 824 (Spotter Reconnaissance) Squadron, flying above HMS *Eagle* in April 1933. At the end of that month the ship sailed fo the China Station, where its aircraft were shore-based at Ka Tak, Hong Kong. The carrier wa originally laid down as a battleship for the Chilean Navy which accounts for the heavy dreadnought lines. The large crane resting on the deck abaft the island was for hoisting seaplanes. (RAF Museum P.101783)

59. The torpedo-equipped Ripons of No. 810 (Torpedo Bomber) Squadron ranged on the flight deck of HMS *Courageous* during the Home Fleet Summer Cruise in May 1933. Six machines have been temporarily repainted in black for the purposes of the manoeuvres, their wing and fuselage roundels having had t white element eliminated. (RA Museum P. 101732)

58▲ 59▼

▲60

▲61 ▼62

60. Blackburn Ripon II S1557 of No. 810 (Torpedo Bomber) Squadron, with its tailskid mounted on wheels for manoeuvring purposes, bears the fleet number '06' on the light blue diagonal fuselage band of HMS *Courageous*. This photograph was taken on 19 December 1933, when the aircraft was temporarily at the Royal Aircraft Establishment, Farnborough, for tests with an experimental wireless installation.

61. The wing-grabbing party runs towards Blackburn Ripon I S1652 of No. 811 (Torpedo Bomber) Squadron as it comes to a halt after landing on the flight deck of HMS *Furious* (whose palisades are erected) around 1934. The fleet number '14', carried in white on a red diagonal fuselage band, is repeated in flags painted on the inner sections of the upper mainplanes, the red and white checks of No. 1 to port and the blue, white and red bands of No 4 to starboard. (RAF Museum P.8314)

62. The Supermarine Seagull V prototype, here bearing the manufacturer's Class B registration 'N-2', served as the prototype for the Walrus and wa later re-serialled K4797. It is

here taking off from HMS *Courageous* during a Home Fleet exercise in March 1934. Piloted by Lieutenant C. John (later to become Admiral of the Fleet Sir Caspar John GCB), it embarked from Lee-on-Solent on 19 February, transferring to the battlecruiser HMS *Renown* on 29 March on completion of the exercise. (RAF Museum)

63. Hawker Osprey Is and IIs of No. 803 (Fleet Fighter) Squadron from HMS *Hermes* in line abreast, around 1934. White fleet numbers are carried on a green fuselage chevron edged with yellow, and the squadron commander's aircraft, K2781 '285', has a green fin. The furthest machine, K2780 '287', was that flown by Lieutenant J. Casson during the piracy affair. The ship was at that time attached to the China Station, the aircraft using Kai Tak, Hong Kong, as a shore base. (FAA Museum)

64. Hawker Nimrods and Ospreys of No. 800 (Fleet Fighter) Squadron and Fairey IIIFs of No. 822 (Spotter Reconnaissance) Squadron lined up at Manston during Channel Exercises in November 1934. All bear the light blue fuselage bands of HMS *Courageous*, and the Hawker aircraft have a similar-coloured bars and diamonds design on the upper wings. (Via A. G. Brown)

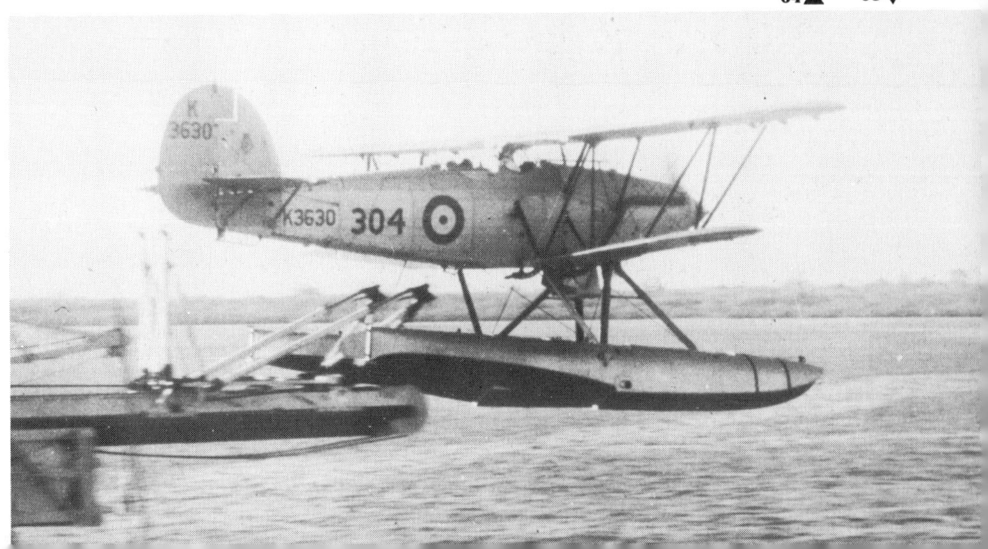

65. Hawker Osprey III K3630 '304', of No. 406 (Fleet Reconnaissance) Flight, piloted by Lieutenant J. W. S. Corbett RN, being catapulted from the cruiser HMS *Emerald* on 31 July 1935. The ship, which was attached to the East Indies Fleet, was then paying a few days' visit to Kilwa Kisiwani, Tanganyika. (Lt Cdr J. W. S. Corbett via FAA Museum)

66. Blackburn Baffin conversion S1473, of No. 811 (Torpedo Bomber) Flight, bears the white fleet number '14' on the diagonal red band of HMS *Furious*. Seen here around 1935, it was given the new fleet number '608' under the revised numbering system introduced shortly afterwards. (RAF Museum P.10661)

67. The second production Blackburn Shark I, K4350, had a cowled Armstrong-Siddeley Tiger engine. The type was first introduced into No. 820 (Spotter Reconnaissance) Squadron at the end of 1934, and this example was photographed the following year bearing the fleet number '738' and the pale blue fuselage band of HMS *Courageous*. (Official)

▲**66** ▼**67**

68. Blackburn Baffin S1553 '45', of 'A' Flight, No. 820 Squadron, parked at Aboukir. The aircraft has the last digit of its fleet number repeated above the upper centre-section in the form of a No. 5 naval flag. This was one of several aircraft from HMS *Courageous*, which sailed to Egypt in August 1935 after the Italians had invaded Abyssinia; in the background can be seen one of the Hawker Ospreys of No. 800 Squadron from the same ship, which also carried the Baffins of No. 810 Squadron and the Fairey Seals of No. 821 Squadron. The carrier sailed home in February 1936 without having seen action. (RAF Museum P. 1765)

69. The lead aircraft for the Jubilee Flypast on 16 July 1936 was Fairey Seal K3519 '804', of No. 823 (Fleet Spotter Reconnaissance) Squadron from HMS *Glorious*. Piloted by Lieutenant Commander C. R. V. Pugh, it carried Rear-Admiral the Hon. Sir Alexander R. M. Ramsey KCVO CB DSO, then Rear-Admiral, Aircraft Carriers. His flag was painted on the black fin of the aircraft for the occasion, the wheel discs being also black.

70. In the spring of 1936 a new aircraft identification system was introduced to replace fleet numbers. This comprised allocations to each flight or squadron of blocks of successive two-letter code combinations. The Supermarine Walruses of No. 715 (Catapult) Flight with the 5th Cruiser Squadron on the China Station adopted 'WM' to 'WX', and K5780 from HMS *Cumberland* is here seen aboard HMS *Eagle* bearing the black code 'WM' on its nose. Across the fin and rudder is a band, probably also black, adorned with the badge of the parent ship. The new coding system was not popular, and in April 1937 it was abolished, very few units having actually adopted it. (FAA Museum)

68▲

69▲ 70▼

▲71

71. Hawker Osprey seaplanes of No. 447 (Catapult) Flight flying over Alexandria harbour in 1936. Aircraft of this unit were flown from ships of the 1st Cruiser Squadron, serving with the Mediterranean Fleet; the nearest machine, K3642 '067', was based aboard HMS *Shropshire*. This unit became No. 711 (Catapult) Flight on 15 July 1936, but K3642 did not survive that long, having crashed and caught fire on 22 May 1936 when it stalled on take-off from Aboukir airfield whilst fitted with a wheeled undercarriage. (RAF Museum P.102755)

▲72 ▼73

72. Seen here around 1936–37, Hawker Osprey I S1696, of No. 803 (Fleet Fighter) Flight, is having its folding wings extended after being brought up from the hangar on the lift of HMS *Hermes*. The carrier has her wind breaks lowered, and the smoke streamer at the bows gives a ready indication of the wind-over-deck. Each aircraft of this squadron had an individual marking on the upper wing centre-section, in this instance a black chevron. The fleet number '290' is painted on a green fuselage chevron, this carrier colour having replaced the white which was used earlier by aircraft from this ship. (RAF Museum)

73. Hawker Nimrod I K2912, of No. 800 (Fleet Fighter) Squadron from HMS *Courageous*, is fished out of the sea off the Isle of Wight, after engine failure led to it making a forced landing astern of the ship on 1 September 1936. The fleet number '120' is carried on a light blue diagonal fuselage band, and the flight colours on the upper wing surfaces are also blue. (FAA Museum)

74. Nimrods and Ospreys of No. 800 (Fleet Fighter) Squadron ranged for take-off aboard HMS *Courageous*, around 1936, with Fairey IIIFs of No. 821 (Spotter Reconnaissance) Squadron ready to follow them. All engines have been started, the wing tips are held back, and a deck crewman lies by each wheel chock ready to move it away. (RAF Museum)

75. Blackburn Baffin S1358 was converted from a Ripon. Originally named the Ripon V, the Baffin had a Bristol Pegasus radial engine in place of the Napier inline engine of its predecessor. This machine, which bears the white fleet number '523' on a light blue diagonal fuselage band, belonged to No. 810 (Torpedo Bomber) Squadron, HMS *Courageous*, around 1936. It was later to be one of a number of its type sold to New Zealand, becoming NZ164 before being relegated to ground instructional use as Inst.19.

76. Numerous examples of the Supermarine Walrus amphibian flying boat served with catapult units aboard battleships and cruisers from 1935 onwards. K8543 is being hoisted by probably HMS *Newcastle*, from which it was flown by No. 712 (Catapult) Flight in 1937. In the background is the destroyer HMS *Skate*. (FAA Museum)

74▲

75▲ 76▼

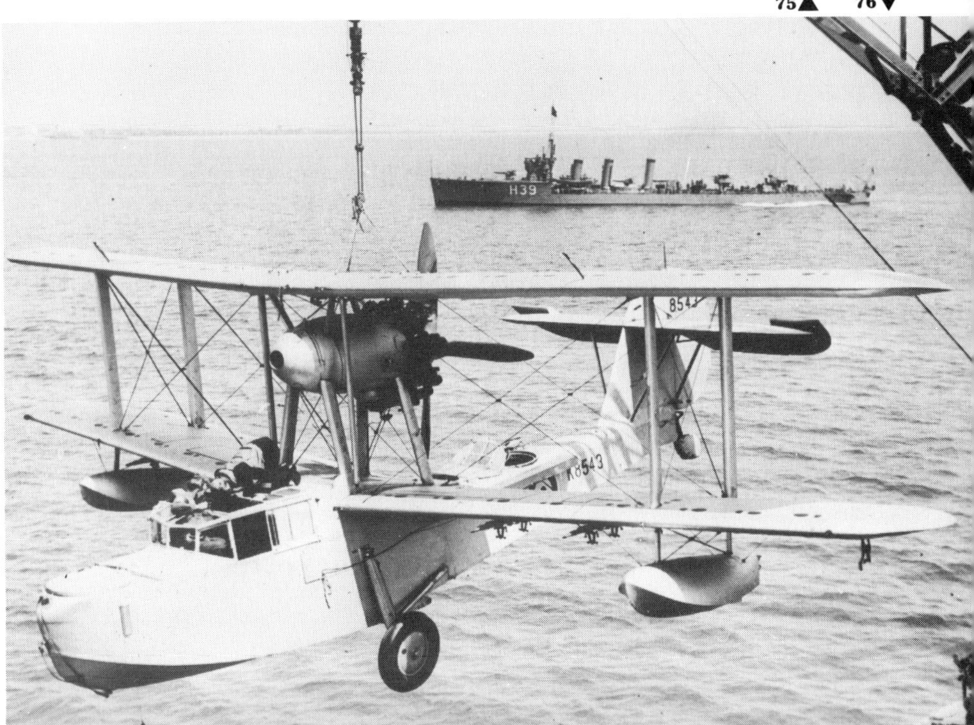

▲77

77. Fairey Seafox K8578 surrounded by a large crowd of native 'helpers'. This example was serving with No. 716 (Catapult) Flight, having been taken aboard the cruiser HMS *Neptune* when she left Portsmouth on 2 September 1937. This photograph could well have been taken on 2 October 1937 when the ship put in to Port Etienne in order to pick up a seaplane in sheltered waters.

78. Blackburn Shark I K5609, of No. 821 (Spotter Reconnaissance) Squadron and temporarily fitted with twin metal floats, is hoisted on to the dockside, in about 1937. It carries the fleet number '684' in white on the light blue diagonal band of HMS *Courageous*. (FAA Museum)

▼78

79. A flight of Fairey Swordfish Is of No. 825 (Torpedo Spotter Reconnaissance) Squadron flying above HMS *Glorious* around 1937–38. The carrier could be distinguished at that time from her sister-ship HMS *Courageous* by the 'W' shaped struts supporting the round-down and after end of the flight deck, these having been fitted during her 1935 refit. The aircraft carried black fleet numbers on a yellow band, the leader also having a black circle on the fin. (RAF Museum P. 103447)

80. Fairey Swordfish I K5990 '584', of No. 813 (Torpedo Spotter Reconnaissance) Squadron from HMS *Eagle*, taxies past two British submarines in Chinese waters around 1937–38. Duties in this area included protecting ships against Chinese pirates. (FAA Museum)

81. Supermarine Walrus K8560, seen here being hoisted around 1938, had the black fleet number '769' painted on the bows. Attached to No. 718 (Catapult) Flight, this aircraft was flown from HMS *Exeter*, one of the vessels in the 8th Cruiser Squadron on the America and West Indies Station, using Bermuda as a shore base. The front tips of the wing flats were probably painted red, and the underside of the hull had a lanolin-based paint applied to keep it watertight. (FAA Museum)

79▲

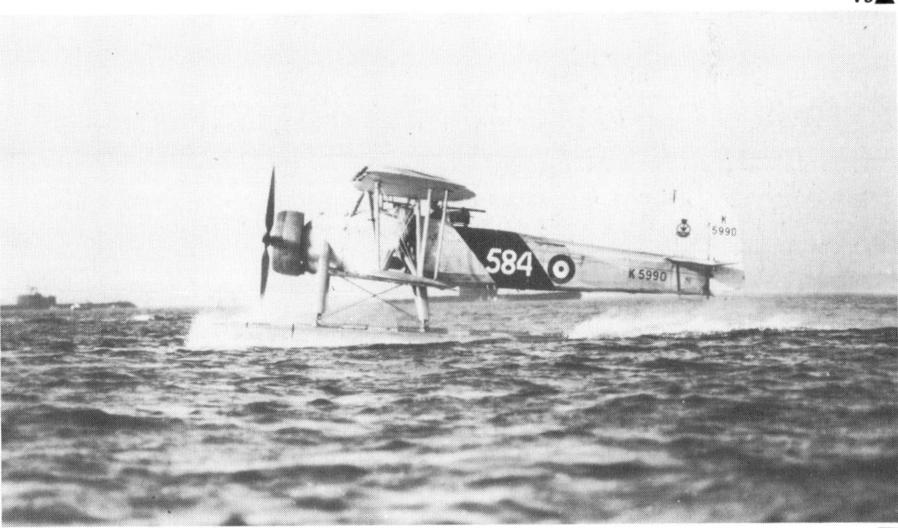

80▲ 81▼

▲82

▲83

82. An accelerated take-off from HMS *Courageous* for torpedo-laden Fairey Swordfish I L2718, of No. 820 (Torpedo Spotter Reconnaissance) Squadron, around June 1938. The fleet number '652' is in white on a light blue diagonal fuselage band. (RAF Museum P.104097)

83. The four Supermarine Walruses of No. 720 (Catapult) Flight on ships of the New Zealand Division used a non-standard type of identification marking, consisting of the black letter/number combinations 'Z1' to 'Z4' painted on the nose. K5774 'Z4', seen here at Fiji in November 1938, is suspended from the crane of HMNZS *Achilles*. (FAA Museum)

84. Swordfish, Ospreys and Nimrods ranged on the deck of the new carrier HMS *Ark Royal* in early 1939, ready for flying of as the ship turns into the wind. This was the first large Royal Navy carrier to be specifically designed and built as such, all previous carriers (with the exception of the small *Hermes*) being conversions. Her displacement of 22,000 tons wa intended to meet a planned international treaty limitation still under negotiation at the time she was laid down. (RAF Museum P.104822)

◀84

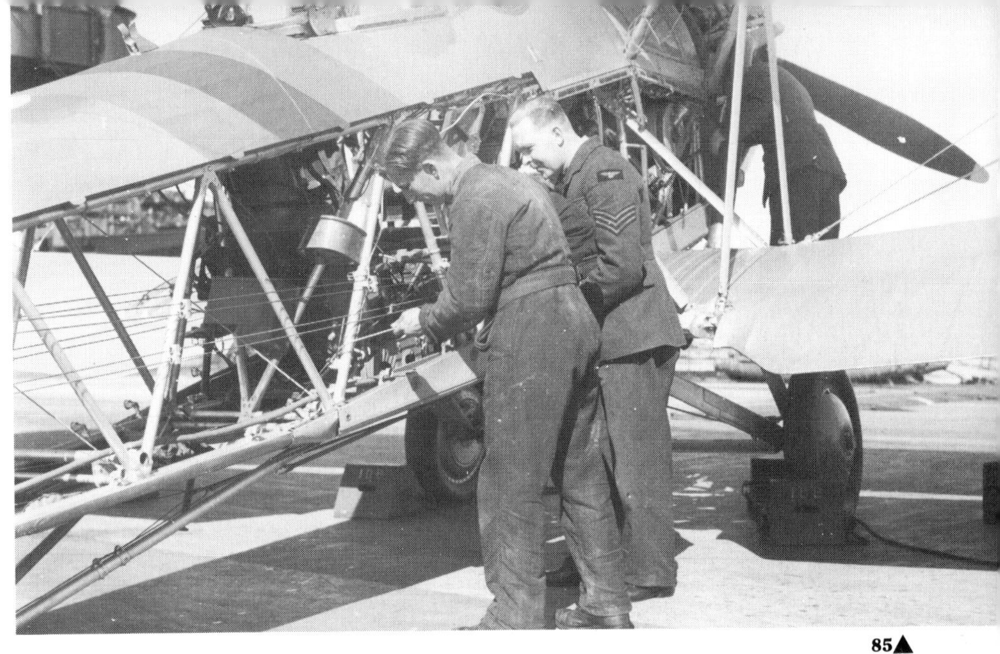

85▲

85. Royal Air Force riggers attached to the Fleet Air Arm test the control wires of a Hawker Osprey of No. 800 (Fleet Fighter) Squadron aboard HMS *Ark Royal* early in 1939; a fitter is working on the engine. All the side panels have been removed while the aircraft is thoroughly checked over. (RAF Museum P.104744)

86. Hawker Osprey K5742 '108' and others of No. 800 (Fleet Fighter) Squadron ranged on the flight deck of HMS *Ark Royal* in early 1939, ready for flying off. Above K5742's tail can be seen a battery of 2pdr pom-pom guns, which would be put to good use against German attackers a few months later. (RAF Museum P.104820)

86▼

▲87 ▼88

▲89

87. Royal Air Force wireless operators attached to the Fleet Air Arm busy themselves inspecting accumulators beneath the engine of a Hawker Osprey of No. 800 (Fleet Fighter) Squadron aboard HMS *Ark Royal*. The photograph was taken while the ship was in dock early in 1939. (RAF Museum P.104741)

88. A classic photograph of Fairey Swordfish I L9781, of No. 820 (Torpedo Spotter Reconnaissance) Squadron, banking above HMS *Ark Royal* in early 1939. This aircraft carries the white fleet number '650' on a blue/red/blue diagonal fuselage band, which was replaced shortly afterwards by the wartime-style call-sign 'A4B'. (RAF Museum P.104829)

89. An active deck scene aboard HMS *Ark Royal* in early 1939, with the Fairey Swordfish of No. 821 (Torpedo Spotter Reconnaissance) Squadron ranged and ready for take-off. Two of the hinged wireless masts can be seen at the side of the ship in the lowered, 'flying' position. The identification colours of this squadron were unique in that, besides a white fleet number carried on a blue/red/blue fuselage band, they carried a tapering horizontal blue band extending forward and aft. (RAF Museum P.104814)

90▲

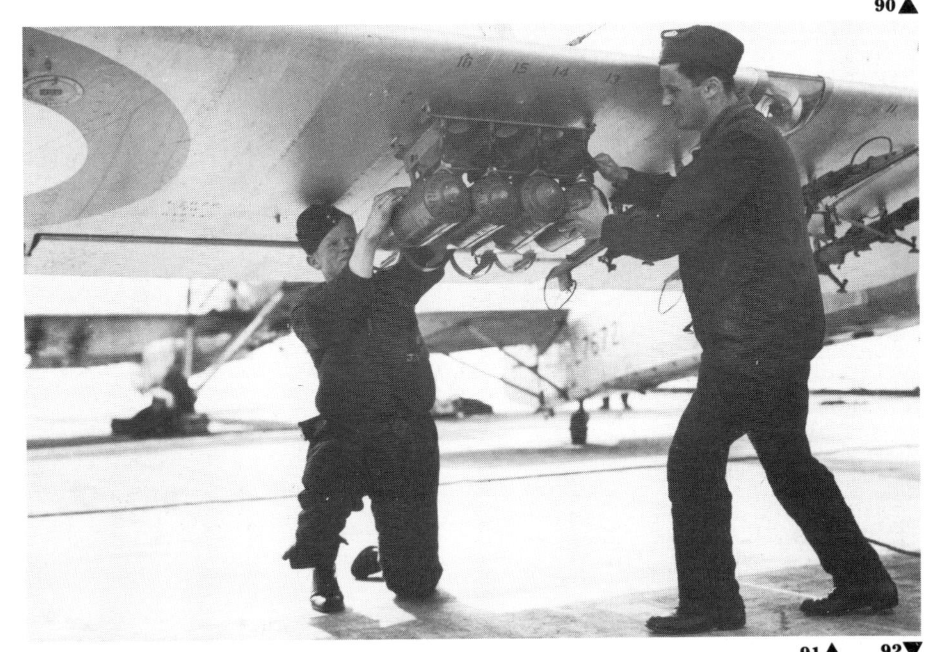

91▲ 92▼

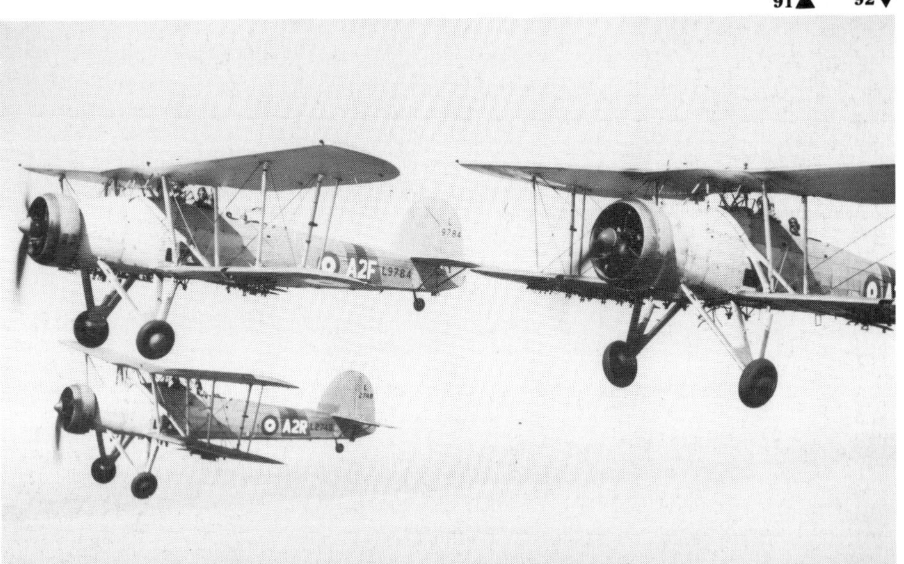

90. Telegraphist air gunners of No. 820 (Torpedo Spotter Reconnaissance) Squadron aboard HMS *Ark Royal* don flying clothing (and a warm scarf) as they stand in front of one of the squadron's Fairey Swordfish Is (L7672 '649') around early 1939. On the fin of this aircraft can be seen the squadron badge, comprising a blue flying fish above blue and white waves. This badge is still in use today, the squadron being currently equipped with Westland Sea King helicopters. (RAF Museum P.104742)

91. Royal Air Force armourers attached to the Royal Navy fix smoke bombs under the wings of Fairey Swordfish I L7672 '649', of No. 820 (Torpedo Spotter Reconnaissance) Squadron aboard HMS *Ark Royal*, in early 1939. (RAF Museum P.104746)

92. A flight of Fairey Swordfish of No. 810 (Torpedo Spotter Reconnaissance) Squadron from HMS *Ark Royal* flying along the south coast of England around May 1939. Squadron call-signs, in this case in the 'A2' range, had just replaced fleet numbers, and are carried in white on a blue/red/blue fuselage band; the latter would shortly be abolished with the adoption of camouflage. (RAF Museum CP.813)

▲93

▲94 ▼95

93. A torpedo is loaded on to a Fairey Swordfish I by Royal Air Force ground crew attached to the Fleet Air Arm. Fitted with a 690hp Bristol Pegasus IIIM3 radial engine, the Swordfish had a top speed of only 139mph but, despite being slow, it had superb deck and flying characteristics and consequently was still in active service at the end of the Second World War, its outdated design notwithstanding. (RAF Museum)

94. A formation of Fairey Swordfish Is of No. 814 (Torpedo Spotter Reconnaissance) Squadron flying over HMS *Ark Royal* in early 1939. Fleet numbers were painted in black aft of the fuselage roundel, the carrier's colours being applied forward of the roundel in the form of a blue/red/blue chevron. This short-lived combination was necessary since the steady increase in the number of operational aircraft carriers had exhausted the range of basic carrier identification colours. (RAF Museum P.104837)

95. Still in peacetime colours, a Blackburn Skua, with flaps down, runs up its engine aboard HMS *Ark Royal*. Just visible to the left in the original print is a destroyer standing by to carry out a rescue if an aircraft should have the misfortune to land in the sea. (Cdr R. N. Everett)

96. Blackburn Skuas of No. 803 (Fleet Fighter) Squadron from HMS *Ark Royal* flying off the south coast of England around June 1939. The nearest machine, L2889, was later transferred to No. 801 Squadron, but was lost on 9 September 1940 when, flying from Hatston, it failed to return from an attack on enemy shipping near Haugesund, Norway. (RAF Museum P.104923)

96▲

·7. The second prototype of the 'airey Seafox light seaplane, een here carrying two small ombs, later served with No. 765 Seaplane Training) Squadron at andbanks, Poole Harbour. This ype saw operational service in he early stages of the Second Vorld War, and one example rovided vital spotting infor- nation during the Battle of the iver Plate towards the end of 939, leading to the scuttling of ie German pocket battleship *raf Spee*. (RAF Museum .105775)

97▲ 98▼

3. Few prewar photographs xist of Gloster Sea Gladiators. iis machine, N5519 of No. 802 'leet Fighter) Squadron, is seen king off from the flight deck of MS *Glorious* some time during e summer of 1939. Its call- gn, 'G6A', borne on a yellow selage chevron, suggests that is was the aircraft of the uadron commander, eutenant Commander G. N. rry RN. The ship was then rving in the Mediterranean. AF Museum P.012201)

The *Fotofax* series

A new range of pictorial studies of military subjects for the modeller, historian and enthusiast. Each title features a carefully-selected set of photographs plus a data section of facts and figures on the topic covered. With line drawings and detailed captioning, every volume represents a succinct and valuable study of the subject. New and forthcoming titles:

Warbirds
F-111 Aardvark
P-47 Thunderbolt
B-52 Stratofortress
Stuka!
Jaguar
US Strategic Air Power: Europe 1942–1945
Dornier Bombers
RAF in Germany

Vintage Aircraft
German Naval Air Service
Sopwith Camel
Fleet Air Arm, 1920–1939
German Bombers of WWI

Soldiers
World War One: 1914
World War One: 1915
World War One: 1916
Union Forces of the American Civil War
Confederate Forces of the American Civil War
Luftwaffe Uniforms
British Battledress 1945–1967 (2 vols)

Warships
Japanese Battleships, 1897–1945
Escort Carriers of World War Two
German Battleships, 1897–1945
Soviet Navy at War, 1941–1945
US Navy in World War Two, 1943–1944
US Navy, 1946–1980 (2 vols)
British Submarines of World War One

Military Vehicles
The Chieftain Tank
Soviet Mechanized Firepower Today
British Armoured Cars since 1945
NATO Armoured Fighting Vehicles
The Road to Berlin
NATO Support Vehicles

The *Illustrated* series

The internationally successful range of photo albums devoted to current, recent and historic topics, compiled by leading authors and representing the best means of obtaining your own photo archive.

Warbirds
US Spyplanes
USAF Today
Strategic Bombers, 1945–1985
Air War over Germany
Mirage
US Naval and Marine Aircraft Today
USAAF in World War Two
B-17 Flying Fortress
Tornado
Junkers Bombers of World War Two
Argentine Air Forces in the Falklands Conflict
F-4 Phantom Vol II
Army Gunships in Vietnam
Soviet Air Power Today
F-105 Thunderchief
Fifty Classic Warbirds
Canberra and B-57
German Jets of World War Two

Vintage Warbirds
The Royal Flying Corps in World War One
German Army Air Service in World War One
RAF between the Wars
The Bristol Fighter
Fokker Fighters of World War One
Air War over Britain, 1914–1918
Nieuport Aircraft of World War One

Tanks
Israeli Tanks and Combat Vehicles
Operation Barbarossa
Afrika Korps
Self-Propelled Howitzers
British Army Combat Vehicles 1945 to the Present
The Churchill Tank
US Mechanized Firepower Today
Hitler's Panzers
Panzer Armee Afrika
US Marine Tanks in World War Two

Warships
The Royal Navy in 1980s
The US Navy Today
NATO Navies of the 1980s
British Destroyers in World War Two
Nuclear Powered Submarines
Soviet Navy Today
British Destroyers in World War One
The World's Aircraft Carriers, 1914–1945
The Russian Convoys, 1941–1945
The US Navy in World War Two
British Submarines in World War Two
British Cruisers in World War One
U-Boats of World War Two
Malta Convoys, 1940–1943

Uniforms
US Special Forces of World War Two
US Special Forces 1945 to the Present
The British Army in Northern Ireland
Israeli Defence Forces, 1948 to the Present
British Special Forces, 1945 to Present
US Army Uniforms Europe, 1944–1945
The French Foreign Legion
Modern American Soldier
Israeli Elite Units
US Airborne Forces of World War Two
The Boer War
The Commandos World War Two to the Present
Victorian Colonial Wars

A catalogue listing these series and other Arms & Armour Press titles is available on request from: Sales Department, Arms & Armour Press, Artillery House, Artillery Row, London SW1P 1RT.